D1000332

THE LOTUS FLOWERS

Also by the author

CLAIMING KIN

THE FORCES OF PLENTY

Ellen Bryant Voigt

THE LOTUS FLOWERS

poems

W · W · NORTON & COMPANY

NEW YORK · LONDON

Epigraph from "1919" by W.B. Yeats. Reprinted with the permission of Macmillan Publishing Company from *Collected Poems* of W.B. Yeats. © 1928 by Macmillan Publishing Company, renewed 1956 by Georgie Yeats. Ellen Bryant Voigt acknowledges the permission of A.P. Watt Limited on behalf of Michael Yeats and Macmillan London Ltd. to quote from "1919" by W.B. Yeats.

"Women, women, what do they want?" (Freud). Translated by Ellen Bryant Voigt.

FIRST EDITION

The text of this book is composed in Souvenir Light, with display type set in Weiss. Composition and manufacturing by the Maple Vail Book Manufacturing Group. Book design by Marjorie J. Flock.

With thanks to the following magazines, in which these poems first appeared:

The American Poetry Review: "Bright Leaf" / *The Atlantic:* "Fairy Tale," "Frog," "The Photograph," "The Storm," "The Wide and Varied World," "The Wish" / *The Iowa Review:* "Equinox" / *Ironwood:* "Feast Day" / *The Nation:* "The Riders," "A Song," "Stone Pond" / *The New Virginia Review:* "Amaryllis," "Under Gemini" / *The New Yorker:* "Dancing with Poets," "The Fence," "Landscape, Dense with Trees," "The Lotus Flowers," "Memorial Day" / *Partisan Review:* "Nightshade" / *Pequod:* "The Pendulum," "The Trust," "The Waterfall" / *Ploughshares:* "The Farmer," "Nocturne," "Short Story," "Visting the Graves" / *The Seneca Review:* "The Chosen," "The Cusp" / *Threepenny Review:* "May" / *TriQuarterly:* "The Last Class" / *Virginia Quarterly Review:* "At the Movie: Virginia, 1956," "The Field Trip," "Good News," "The Visitor."

And particular thanks to Michael Ryan for his support and suggestions.

Library of Congress Cataloging-in-Publication Data
Voigt, Ellen Bryant, 1943–
The Lotus flowers.

I. Title.
PS3572.034L6 1987 811'.54 86–23922

ISBN 0-393-02445-8

W. W. Norton & Company, Inc., 500 Fifth Avenue, New York, N. Y. 10110
W. W. Norton & Company Ltd., 37 Great Russell Street, London WC1B 3NU

1 2 3 4 5 6 7 8 9 0

For Fran, and for Louise

Contents

I

II

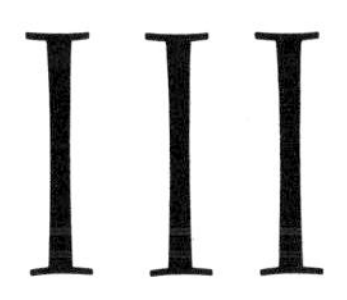

Man is in love and loves what vanishes.

—*W. B. Yeats*

I

The Last Class

Put this in your notebooks:
All verse is occasional verse.
In March, trying to get home, distracted
and impatient at Gate 5 in the Greyhound station,
I saw a drunk man bothering a woman.
A poem depends on its detail
but the woman had her back to me,
and the man was just another drunk,
black in this case, familiar, dirty.
I moved past them both, got on the bus.

There is no further action to report.
The man is not a symbol. If what he said to her
touches us, we are touched by a narrative
we supply. What he said was, "I'm sorry,
I'm sorry," over and over, "I'm sorry,"
but you must understand he frightened the woman,
he meant to rob her of those few quiet
solitary moments sitting down,
waiting for the bus, before she headed home
and probably got supper for her family,
perhaps in a room in Framingham,
perhaps her child was sick.

My bus pulled out, made its usual turns
and parted the formal gardens from the Common,
both of them camouflaged by snow.
And as it threaded its way to open road,
leaving the city, leaving our sullen classroom,
I postponed my satchel of your poems
and wondered who I am to teach the young,
having come so far from honest love of the world;
I tried to recall how it felt

to live without grief; and then I wrote down
a few tentative lines about the drunk,
because of an old compulsion to record,
or sudden resolve not to be self-absorbed
and full of dread—

I wanted to salvage
something from my life, to fix
some truth beyond all change, the way
photographers of war, miles from the front,
lift print after print into the light,
each one further cropped and amplified,
pruning whatever baffles or obscures,
until the small figures are restored
as young men sleeping.

Visiting the Graves

All day we travel from bed to bed, our children
clutching homemade bouquets
of tulips and jonquils, hyacinth,
handfuls of yellow salad from the fields.
In Pittsylvania County our dead face east,
my great-grandfather and his sons facing
what is now a stranger's farm.
One great-uncle chose a separate hill,
an absence in the only photograph.
Under the big oak, we fumble for his name
and the names of sisters scattered like coins.
But here is my father, near the stone
we watched him weep beside for twenty years.
And my mother beside him, the greenest slab of grass.
By horse, it was hours to Franklin County,
to Liberty Christian Church where her mother lies.
The children squabble in the car, roll on the velvet
slope of the churchyard, pout or laugh as we point out
the gap in the mountain where *her* mother's grave
is underwater, the lake lapping the house, the house
still standing like a tooth. We tell them how
we picked huckleberries from the yard,
tell them what a huckleberry is, but the oldest
can't keep straight who's still alive, the smallest
wants her flowers back—who can blame them,
this far from home, tired of trying
to climb a tree of bones. They fall asleep
halfway down the road, and we fall silent, too,
who were taught to remember and return,
my sister is driving, I'm in the back,
the sky before us a broken field of cloud.

Feast Day

If you wanted to hang a sprig of mistletoe,
you had to shoot it down from the tree. Summers,
with so much dense proliferation at the horizon,
the eye was caught by weed and bush, grapes
sprawling on a low fence, hedgerows of wild rose
or privet hedge, a snarl of honeysuckle, blackberry
along the red gash the road made, and kudzu overtaking
the banks, the rotting logs, a burnt-out barn.
But in winter, from a distance, scanning the hills,
you could easily spot a clump of mistletoe
in the high oak, the topmost branches—
like a nest against the gray sky,
and closer, the only green thing left in the black tree.
After Advent, having tied the wreath of running cedar
to the door and whacked a blue-tipped cedar
out of the field; having unearthed the white potatoes
and the yams, brought down pears and peaches from the shelf;
having sweated all the sugar from the sorghum
and plucked the doves; having long since
slaughtered the hog and hung it by the heels in a nearby tree;
having boiled and scraped the bristles, slabbed the ribs,
packed the hams in salt, rinsed and stuffed the gut,
plunged the knuckles into brine, having eaten the testicles
and ground the snout with any remaining parts to make a cheese,
you went upcountry with your gun.
O mild Christ,
the long plank table is spread with wealth
and everyone is gathered. The father puts aside
the quarrel with his one remaining son, the mother
wipes an eye on her apron, the daughters hush,
the cousins cease their cruel competition.

On the table, the brass centerpiece is heaped
with the brilliant red beads of pyracantha,
thorn of fire, torn from a low shrub beside the house;
and lifted above them—emblem of peace, emblem of affection—
the fleshy leaves of mistletoe, bearing its few pearls,
its small inedible berry.

The Photograph

Black as a crow's wing was what they said
about my mother's hair. Even now,
back home, someone on the street
will stop me to recall my mother, how beautiful she was,
first among her sisters.
In the photograph, her hair
is a spill of ink below the white beret,
a swell of dark water. And her eyes as dark,
her chin lifted, that brusque defining posture
she had just begun in her defense.
Seventeen, on her own,
still a shadow in my father's longing—nothing
the camera could record foretold
her restlessness, the years of shrill
unspecified despair, the clear reproach
of my life, just beginning.

The horseshoe hung in the neck of the tree sinks
deeper into heartwood every season.
Sometimes I hear the past
hum in my ear, its cruel perfected music,
as I turn from the stove
or stop to braid my daughter's thick black hair.

The Riders

He asks for little, so great
is his despair. At the crest
of the white hill, he waits
near the fire, holding the reins
of his expensive sled. The girls
giggle and flirt, winding and unwinding
their patterned scarves—a grown man
wants their attention. One of them
finally edges toward him,
as other children appear
and disappear, plying the hill.
There is no moon, his face
is lit by snow. Although she cannot
name what she feels, already
she understands the terms
of these arrangements:
from her, a rudimentary kindness,
and in exchange, the polished track,
the dull self falling away.

The Chosen

1

You cannot see the horns from where you sit,
only another row in common black.
When their clear melody
comes in to represent a grieving heart,
it will do so as a brook, rushing over stones,
approximates a flock of birds rising,
or as the peacock sounds like human speech.
Now the empty instruments
are raised. I open the first cadenza,
the weight of my arms and shoulders
striking the keys, keys in turn
hammering the hidden strings,
driving triumph from the concert grand:
and when the multiple voices join, when the horns,
in that famous passage, surprise you, it seems
we've touched the vocal center of the world.
The audience a blur on my right,
musicians on my left, I face into the wings,
across the keyboard and its broad extension.
Playing, I have no more choices
to be made. Playing,
I am no one.

2

A child sits on the round, embroidered stool,
screwed to its full height, a box
over the pedals for her feet.
The wooden lip is raised and she taps
at the row of teeth. Suddenly, a passage
from memory, and a bird startles
into its territorial cry; then
she hesitates, tries an accidental—
this is the hard part, the new part,
she doesn't like to make mistakes.
Thinking his opinion matters,
the teacher clicks the rhythm
with a pencil, but I would like
to move those fingers by remote control,
to make her go ahead, take a chance,
play *something.* The piano itself
seems to grow impatient, waiting,
as the tired upright waited for me
in the damp Victorian parlor, a secret
under its fringed shawl, the songs
in the fat book almost in reach—

3

I didn't simply stop getting better.
Pushing a stone, one cannot stop on a hill.
The dancer's legs, the poised embouchure
want to be part of a sleeping animal.

I can still name the train's declining note,
the pitch growing flat as it recedes;
on the street, in a crowd, I can duplicate
the chord implied beneath a random noise—

so much music in the universe!
In the practice halls, or in the deadened
air of their small carrels, apart from us,
musicians are laboring, themselves
the instruments—
                                        it is a service;
and like the tired wife who never meant
to foreswear her chosen joy, I merely
gave a lesser portion of myself,

poco a poco until my hands
no longer strained against the leash; and then
no longer could outrun my eye; and soon, soon,
I could not even bear to listen.

The Trust

Something was killing sheep
but it was sheep this dog attended on the farm—
a black-and-white border collie, patrolling his fold
like a parish priest. The second time the neighbor came,
claiming to have spotted the dog at night, a crouched figure
slithering toward the pen on the far side of the county,
the farmer let him witness how the dog,
alert and steady, mended the frayed
edge of the flock, the clumped sheep calm
as they drifted together along the stony hill.
But still more sheep across the glen were slaughtered,
and the man returned more confident. This time,
the master called his dog forward,
and stroking the eager head, prized open the mouth to find,
wound around the base of the back teeth—squat molars
the paws can't reach to clean—small coils of wool,
fine and stiff, like threads from his own jacket.
So he took down the rifle from the rack
and shot the dog and buried him,
his best companion in the field for seven years.
Once satisfied, the appetite is never dulled again.
Night after night, its sweet insistent promise
drives the animal under the rail fence and miles away
for a fresh kill; and with guilty cunning brings him back
to his familiar charges, just now stirring in the early light,
brings him home to his proud husbandry.

The Farmer

In the still-blistering late afternoon,
like currying a horse the rake
circled the meadow, the cut grass ridging
behind it. This summer, if the weather held,
he'd risk a second harvest after years
of reinvesting, leaving fallow.
These fields were why he farmed—
he walked the fenceline like a man in love.
The animals were merely what he needed: cattle
and pigs; chickens for a while; a drayhorse,
saddle horses he was paid to pasture—
an endless stupid round
of animals, one of them always hungry, sick, lost,
calving or farrowing, or waiting slaughter.

When the field began dissolving in the dusk,
he carried feed down to the knoll,
its clump of pines, gate, trough, lick, chute
and two gray hives; leaned into the Jersey's side
as the galvanized bucket filled with milk;
released the cow and turned to the bees.
He'd taken honey before without protection.
This time, they could smell something
in his sweat—fatigue? impatience,
although he was a stubborn, patient man?
Suddenly, like flame, they were swarming over him.
He rolled in the dirt, manure and stiff hoof-prints,
started back up the path, rolled in the fresh hay—
refused to run, which would have pumped
the venom through him faster—passed the oaks
at the yard's edge, rolled in the yard, reached
the kitchen, and when he tore off his clothes
crushed bees dropped from him like scabs.

For a week he lay in the darkened bedroom.
The doctor stopped by twice a day—
the hundred stings "enough to kill an ox,
enough to kill a younger man." What saved him
were the years of smaller doses—
like minor disappointments,
instructive poison, something he could use.

A Song

Now I am calm. It seems that nothing
can make me feel the same exhausting pain.

What is another's harrowing to me?
Grief is not a lake,

I am miles at sea, miles
from the moving figures—

Why are they calling out?
They cluster at land's edge as though

the stony promontory,
where they had just been standing,

were sheared away.
If they are frightened,

if they also grieve,
let them comfort one another,

I cannot help them, I am riding
each enormous wave of this absence

that knows no further shore.

Short Story

My grandfather killed a mule with a hammer,
or maybe with a plank, or a stick, maybe
it was a horse—the story varied
in the telling. If he was planting corn
when it happened, it was a mule, and he was plowing
the upper slope, west of the house, his overalls
stiff to the knees with red dirt, the lines
draped behind his neck.
He must have been glad to rest
when the mule first stopped mid-furrow;
looked back at where he'd come, then down
to the brush along the creek he meant to clear.
No doubt he noticed the hawk's great leisure
over the field, the crows lumped
in the biggest elm on the opposite hill.
After he'd wiped his hatbrim with his sleeve,
he called to the mule as he slapped the line
along its rump, clicked and whistled.

My grandfather was a slight, quiet man,
smaller than most women, smaller
than his wife. Had she been in the yard,
seen him heading toward the pump now,
she'd pump for him a dipper of cold water.
Walking back to the field, past the corncrib,
he took an ear of corn to start the mule,
but the mule was planted. He never cursed
or shouted, only whipped it, the mule
rippling its backside each time
the switch fell, and when that didn't work
whipped it low on its side, where it's tender,
then cross-hatched the welts he'd made already.
The mule went down on one knee,

and that was when he reached for the blown limb,
or walked to the pile of seasoning lumber; or else,
unhooked the plow and took his own time to the shed
to get the hammer.
By the time I was born,
he couldn't even lift a stick. He lived
another fifteen years in a chair,
but now he's dead, and so is his son,
who never meant to speak a word against him,
and whom I never asked what his father
was planting and in which field,
and whether it happened before he married,
before his children came in quick succession,
before his wife died of the last one.
And only a few of us are left
who ever heard that story.

Stone Pond

Driving over the limit
on a mountain road,
the mist rising, Stone Pond
white with ice and white mist
inside its circle
of birch and black fir:

driving home after
seeing friends, the radio
complicitous and loud,
Beethoven's braided musical line,
a sonata I recall
playing well:

passing the tiny houses
on the hillside, woodsmoke
rising among the budded trees,
then passing within inches
of someone's yard: I circle
Stone Pond, and despair

seems like something I can set aside.
The road bends again, the morning
burns through the mist.
Sufficient joy—
what should I have done to make it last?

II

The Visitor

Every summer, after the slender dogwood by the porch
has dropped its scalloped blossoms, my sister
moves back into the carcass of our house.
Most of the old belongings are disbursed,
most of the photographs, the lamps, the quilts,
the small unraveling stool.
And there's a different smell—
Some other kind of soap in the yellow bathroom,
some other dish simmering on the stove.
Upstairs, in the room we shared,
wasps crawl undisturbed across the pane.
Still, my sister says
she feels my father's presence everywhere—
among the trees and bushes he had planted,
the billiard-cloth of grass she cuts and mends.
After midnight, he turns the light on
in the living room; and once, at his usual waking,
before daybreak could have lit the kitchen,
she heard his spoon chime against his cup.
But not my mother—
not on the glassed-in porch,
not beside the single strand of roses.

My sister thinks it's natural that she comes,
that she stays through August, keeping up
the hardwood floors. Away from her grown children
she sings in the choir, empties another closet,
cultivates the bluebirds in their boxes.
When she calls, her news is either weather
or the birds, it is so quiet there.
But sometimes I hear her hesitate on the phone,
as though to tell me something, or to ask—

Then she is adult again, reports
a new house on the road and more trees cleared.
"Try to get home," is what she says,
the closed vowel encompassing
our set of inland islands: ragged plug
of the Southern map, the house and yard
centered in the green voluptuous fields,
and all of my childhood, pocked reef
floating within me, relic of past eruption
now cooled, now temperate, populous, isolate,
from which I venture further and further
into this life, like a swimmer
still in training, aiming
for the mainland in the distance.

The Wide and Varied World

Women, women, what do they want?

The first ones in the door of the plant-filled office
were the twins, fresh from the upper grades,
their matched coats dangling open.
And then their more compliant brother, leading
the dear stuffed tottering creature—amazing
that she could lift her leg high enough
to cross the threshold to the waiting room.
Then the woman, the patient, carrying the baby
in an infant seat, his every inch of flesh
swaddled against the vicious weather.
Once inside, how skillfully the mother
unwound the many layers—
and now so quickly
must restore them: news from the lab
has passed through the nurse's sliding window.
The youngest, strapped again into his shell,
fusses for the breast, the twins tease their sister,
the eight-year-old looks almost wise as his mother
struggles into her coat with one hand and with the other
pinches his sweaty neck, her hissed threats
swarming his face like flies.
Now she's gone.
The women who remain don't need to speak.
Outside, snow falls in the streets
and quiet hills, and seems, in the window,
framed by the room's continuous greenery,
to obliterate the wide and varied world.
We half-smile, half-nod to one another.
One returns to her magazine.
One shifts gently to the right arm
her sleeping newborn, unfurls the bud of its hand.

One of us takes her turn in the inner office
where she submits to the steel table
and removes from her body its stubborn wish.
We want what you want, only
we have to want it more.

The Field Trip

This time they're thirteen, no longer
interested in the trillium on the path but in each other,
though they will not say so. Only the chaperone
lingers at the adder's tongue,
watching the teacher trail the rest uphill
to where the dense virginal forest thins and opens.
At the clearing, she tells them to be still and mute
and make a list of what they see and hear.
A girl asks if she should also list
the way she feels—she's the one
who'll cite the shadow on the lake below.
The others sprawl on gender-separate rocks
except for the smart-ass, perched
on the cliff-edge, inviting front-page photos—
PICNIC MARRED BY TRAGEDY. From time to time,
in the midst of the day's continual lunch,
as the students read the lists their teacher edits,
the boy swears and stretches—
he is in fact fourteen, doing seventh grade
a second time, this same assignment
also a second time. Pressed, he says
he sees exactly what he saw before—ponds, rocks, trees—
shouting it back from the same vantage point
out on the twelve-inch ledge,
Long Pond a ragged puddle underneath him;
and what he shouts grows more and more
dangerously insubordinate as he leans
more and more dramatically over the edge.
But he is, after all, the first to spot the hawk;
and it is, looking down on it, amazing. The others
gather near the unimpeded view,
together, finally, standing on this bluff
overlooking three natural ponds, hearing the wind

ruffle the cedar fringe, watching the hawk
float along the thermals like a leaf.
And for a moment, belittled by indifferent wilderness,
you want to praise the boy, so much does he resemble
if not the hawk then the doomed shrub
fanned against the rockface there beside him,
rooted in a fissure in the rock.
But soon the hero swings back up to earth,
the group divides. Just like that
they're ready for home, tired of practicing:
sixteen children, two adults, and one
bad boy who carved a scorpion on his arm.

Nocturne

Through the clotted street and down
the alley to the station, the halting
rhythm of the bus disrupts her dream
and makes the broad blond fields of grain
yield to an agitated harbor,
whales nuzzling flank to flank.
Now the bus settles in its gate.
She wakes, smoothes her stockings, gathers
her packages; a nervous woman,
she passes the subway's deep stairs
and aims for the Public Garden: a few ducks
in the shallow murk of the pond, a few bikes,
the labeled trees, the low voltage of the pigeons' moan,
the last light doled out to penthouses on the roofline
where someone shifts an ottoman with his slipper.
This is not the red heart of the city
but its veined, unblinking eye,
her image fixed within the green iris.
Across the avenue, up the blank sidestreet,
the door is locked, those locks her talismen.
She stalls a moment, as a cautious animal pauses
before it is absorbed by foliage—she is alone at dusk
in the emptying corridors of the park. Nearby
a man flattens the clipped grass.
He knows each coin, the currency of faces.
Trailing her from the bus, deft as a cab
in the dense streets, as a dog on the broad common,
he's neither hungry nor afraid, a man with a knife
evolving coolly from the traffic of strangers.
Whereas the violence in nature is just,
beasts taking their necessary flesh,
the city is capricious, releasing brute
want from the body's need where it was housed.

Fairy Tale

The wronged spirit brought the child
a basket of riches:
two parents, justice and mercy;
a beauty both stunning and organic;
fame beyond the wide walls of the castle;
and intelligence, lying like an asp
at the bottom of the basket.
With this last gift she could discern
the flaw in nature
and all of nature's fruits.

Thus she came to her
majority already skilled,
having pressed bright flowers
to a film, having memorized
the verses of the day.
For months, she did not eat,
she did not traffic with the agencies
of change: she had cast her will entirely

against decay. Even when
the wild tangle emerged
from the careful lawns, and ebony birds
came down from the woods
to roost in the chiseled turrets
and foul the court, she would not stir
nor in any way disturb
the triumph that would greet the shallow prince:
a soul unencumbered
in a neutral body.

Under Gemini

This morning, as if striping the lower field
were not enough, sun flooded the south windows
at an angle, dissolving the glass
dividing the plants inside from plants outside
where almost all that blooms is blooming.
So finally I opened all the doors,
unstoppered the upstairs windows and swept away
the delicate crisp husks of flies, the dark
accumulation of the winter. And now
you're splashing the children
with the hose, urging me out into the sun,
as I sit in the shade of the porch under the eaves
where spiders do their work—
symmetrical hammocks and flannel sacks of eggs.
Have you noticed they always move
in increments, from bush to tree to post:
even when they fly, they fall on a tether or make
a lateral swing in the wind—unlike birds, light-bellied
swallows with forked tails and ruddered swifts, descending
from the barn in open air, free-fall, snatching
flies on the wing—summer calls us
to be birds, calls us to abandon.
When Orpheus heard the mermaids sing, he sang louder.
It's right that I wait here with the spiders
growing larger, slower, shrewder
at the target's edge.

Good News

Not smart, not pretty, not especially kind,
one of a million sparrows in God's eye,
she sits in a middle pew this hot
second Sunday in July, All Day Meeting
and eating on the grounds. Home for the day,
wearing a fuchsia dress and precarious smile
she looks somehow fallen but unused,
a peony dismantling on the bush.
As the preacher chides and harrows his drowsy flock
she studies the large mural spread behind him:
their savior dressed in light; eleven choral faces;
and one who's looking, always, down and away.
Through the open door, the open windows
with leaded hillsides flecked with sheep,
no breeze comes in from heaven
to stir the damp curls along her neck
so she moves her paper fan with the languorous
motion of the wrist a Fiji Islander
might use to sway a frond—
                                        Outside, a bird
flutes among the lilies. The cobbled tables
stand between the white church and the graves,
nothing left of chicken and pie, biscuits and lemonade,
nothing left of the women who dished it up
in feathered hats, or the men in shirtsleeves
with their braces showing, boys chasing beneath the oaks
and girls in white piqué and patent shoes, their hair
already wet from the blessed river—as if snatched
out of the yard, they've gone inside
to blink and nod, and swept among them,
this almost unfamiliar single woman, who rustled
from group to group, balancing a tiny plate of food.

Near her, in the aisle, as though arranged,
a thick fluorescent bug struggles and whirs.
And below the windows' many fractured Christs,
the broad metal fans that stir the ceiling, she sees
it isn't dawn in the painting, as she thought,
but dusk and deepening gloom,

as now, in the church,
where the widow to her right with strict gray hair,
the deacons and the choir are standing, the hymn
is gathering speed and urgency, everybody's
singing out for Jesus! The preacher
punctuates the crowd with invitation—Jesus!
Who has saved the sullen grocer at the back,
a farmer and his wife, a naughty child—
Jesus!—and they file forward, happy to be chosen,
but still the preacher's murmuring,
Jesus with the leper, Jesus weeping.
His brow is cool and calm; he has the poor
lost disciple's darkened face, he has the lean
body of the boy who boxes fruit, he holds the only
key to the grave, and she is lovely, rising now,
descending the aisle toward the one who loves her.

Amaryllis

Having been a farmer's daughter
she didn't want to be a farmer's wife, didn't want
the smell of ripe manure in all his clothes,
the corresponding flies in her kitchen,
a pail of slop below the sink,
a crate of baby chicks beside the stove, piping
beneath their bare lightbulb, cows calling at the gate
for him to come, cows standing in the chute
as he crops their horns with his long sharp shears.
So she nagged him toward a job in town;
so she sprang from the table, weeping, when he swore;
so, after supper, she sulks over her mending
as he unfolds his pearl pocketknife
to trim a callus on his palm.
Too much like her mother, he says, not knowing
any other reason why she spoils the children,
or why he comes in from the combine with his wrenches
to find potatoes boiled dry in their pot,
his wife in the parlor on the bench
at her oak piano—not playing
you understand, just sitting like a fern
in that formal room.
So much time to think,
these long hours: like her mother,
each night she goes to bed when her husband's tired,
gets up when he gets up, and in between tries
not to move, listening to the sleep of this good man
who lies beside and over her. So much time alone,
since everything he knows is practical.
Just this morning, he plunged an icepick
into the bloated side of the cow unable to rise,
dying where it fell, its several stomachs having failed—
too full, he said, of sweet wet clover.

Nightshade

The dog lay under the house, having crawled
back beyond the porch, bellying
beneath the joists through rocks and red dirt
to the cool stone foundation where it died
as the children called and sobbed;
and now their father had to wrench it out,
the one he had been breaking to handle birds.

This was a man of strictest moderation,
who had heard a dash of strychnine in its meat
could be a tonic for a dog, an extra edge.
He loved that dog, and got the dosage wrong.
And I loved my father—
I was among the children looking on—
and for years would not forgive him:

without pure evil in the world,
there was no east or west, no polestar
and no ratifying dove. I sat inside
the small white house for hours,
deaf to the world, playing my two songs,
one in a major, the other in a sad, minor key.

At the Movie: Virginia, 1956

This is how it was:
they had their own churches, their own schools,
schoolbuses, football teams, bands and majorettes,
separate restaurants, in all the public places
their own bathrooms, at the doctor's
their own waiting room, in the *Tribune*
a column for their news, in the village
a neighborhood called Sugar Hill,
uneven rows of unresponsive houses
that took the maids back in each afternoon—
in our homes used the designated door,
on Trailways sat in the back, and at the movie
paid at a separate entrance, stayed upstairs.
Saturdays, a double feature drew the local kids
as the town bulged, families surfacing
for groceries, medicine and wine,
the black barber, white clerks in the stores—crowds
lined the sidewalks, swirled through the courthouse yard,
around the stone soldier and the flag,

and still I never *saw* them on the street.
It seemed a chivalric code
laced the milk: you'd try not to look
and they would try to be invisible.
Once, on my way to the creek,
I went without permission to the tenants'
log cabin near the barns, and when Aunt Susie
opened the door, a cave yawned, and beyond her square,
leonine, freckled face, in the hushed interior,
Joe White lumbered up from the table, six unfolding
feet of him, dark as a gun-barrel, his head bent
to clear the chinked rafters, and I caught
the terrifying smell of sweat and grease,
smell of the woodstove, nightjar, straw mattress—

This was rural Piedmont, upper south;
we lived on a farm but not in poverty.
When finally we got our own TV, the evening news
with its hooded figures of the Ku Klux Klan
seemed like another movie—*King Solomon's Mines,*
the serial of Atlantis in the sea.
By then I was thirteen,
and no longer went to movies to see movies.
The downstairs forged its attentions forward,
toward the lit horizon, but leaning a little
to one side or the other, arranging the pairs
that would own the county, stores and farms, everything
but easy passage out of there—
and through my wing-tipped glasses the balcony
took on a sullen glamor: whenever the film
sputtered on the reel, when the music died
and the lights came on, I swiveled my face
up to where they whooped and swore,
to the smoky blue haze and that tribe
of black and brown, licorice, coffee,
taffy, red oak, sweet tea—

wanting to look, not knowing how to see,
I thought it was a special privilege
to enter the side door, climb the stairs
and scan the even rows below—trained bears
in a pit, herded by the stringent rule,
while they were free, lounging above us,
their laughter pelting down on us like trash.

The Storm

After trimming the split trunk of our tallest maple,
we drove along the cluttered road to see
the other damage. On the next high ground,
the neighbors' white frame house was still intact
but their porch was lined in black—like silk, that soft
when we touched it—a jagged hole where the switchbox
used to be, where lightning entered. Indoors,
it had traced a map on the walls
as it traveled the wires behind the walls,
throwing out at every socket fists of fire only inches
from where they sat. No one had been hurt, no one
shocked or burned, but each needed
to tell us what had happened, still figuring
whether to count their luck as bad or good.

We took the long way back to check the creek
loosened from its channel into the fields,
crowding the cattle to an upper ridge,
the young sycamores along the bank
shorter now by half, forking
at water level, and the water red as rust,
swift, swirling the whipped limbs of the willow-oaks,
grazing the concrete bridge and full of trash.
My father explained the bloated lumps
as logs, or broken fence, and pointed out
occasional shimmering arrows at the surface—
something alive and swimming with the current—

trying to make it all seem natural,
as my mother had calmed us
in the noise and flash and passion
we'd shuddered through the night before.

But already a smell was rising from the new river,
the bottomland, the small lost animals it swallowed.
And we were learning risk and consequence:
in the neighbors' yard
strips of rubber draping trees and grass,
the poles unattached, the central silver cord
simply missing, that carried power in.

The Cusp

So few birds—the ones that winter through
and the geese migrating through the empty fields,
fording the cropped, knuckled stalks of corn:
all around us, all that's green's suppressed,
and in the brooding wood, the bare trees,
shorn of leaves or else just shy of leaves,
make a dark estate beneath low clouds
that have the look of stubborn snow.

In a purely scientific exercise—
say you came from the moon, or returned
like Lazarus, blinking from the cave—
you wouldn't know if winter's passed or now beginning.
The bank slopes up, the bank slopes down to the ditch.
Would it help if I said grieving has an end?
Would it matter if I told you this is spring?

The Pendulum

One-third of the house is hanging in the air,
or seems to hang, seems ready to buckle
the six slender jacks underneath—we had to correct
two hundred years of shifting on this hill,
the sills laid in sand and left there, four warped timbers
that frame us as we sleep, frost
pressing every winter on every wall, so far away
from the mild Virginia evenings, the doves calling softly
in the field, and my childhood house, its mild human voices.
In June, in my garden, hearing a dove
across the wooded swell—the first I'd heard
in this northern latitude—I realized that nothing
is left to pull me back there but the graves; and like an exile
finally turning inland from the shore, I could admit
I'm here to stay.
So we exposed the rotten wood
from outside in, the vast machine laboring in the yard,
its prehistoric hand surprisingly agile, tender; and at night
can feel that end of the house
shuddering up to pitch on the iron rods, as though we had
released it, had removed the weights from the swimmer's feet;
and the awful dreams have started once again, although
I wake to find the children undisturbed. Do they know
how soon the dirt mounded on the grass
will be shoveled back against the new foundation,
the cellarhole tucked in? Already, stone by stone
the Polish mason sets us right—not on the earth
but in it, level where the land is not,
squared where it slopes away and plumb to a rule, the line
that ties this planet to its star: a line made visible
by the string he hangs from the underside of the house,
its dependent metal cone an ornament, a pendulum
that sways, slows, grows perfectly still
to mark the footings here, and here, and here.

Frog

can't help herself, goes in and out of water
all day long. The reed wags like a finger,
the slick patch of algae shrugs and stretches—
Make up your mind.
They have the luxury of just one life.
Frog would like to venture into the weeds, or further still,
but her skin dries, too much open air is like a poison.
Underwater, confident again, Frog
keeps her legs together
to imitate the missing tail, circles the long trout,
plunges down to sweet familiar ooze.
But Frog is always too soon out of breath
and must return to the bright element
where the other land-fish line the banks,
huge and slow, picking their teeth. Close by,
in the blurred trees, new rivals have been hatching.
Frog takes up her perch where the linked bubbles
decorate the wet hem of the pond.
She sits and sits, like a clod of grass, her eyeballs
fixed and glassy, the slim tongue uncurls, curls
in her mouth: although she cannot fly
she eats what does. And then,
staring down into her losses, into the pool
that swaddled her among her mute companions,
Frog fills her throat with air and sings.

III

The Waterfall

Meeting after twenty years apart,
I ask my friend to give me back myself
at nineteen, but he can't, or won't:
Sunny, he says, and quick to speak your mind.
Then he asks if he has aged,
if he looks the same—who had always seemed
so satisfied, past need, past harm.
At every stop we stare at each other,
returning to the other's face as though
it were a wind-rucked pond we hope will clear.
And slowly, as we spiral up the mountain,
looking for landmarks, the road
a narrow shelf on the wooded slopes, I realize
he's terrified of me; and since he cannot yet
know who I am, begin to see myself as I was then:
implacable:

                    but that's not the word he flung at me
beside the shaded pool, the blanket smoothed,
the picnic barely opened.
That was years ago;
now we have the usual pleasantries,
trade photographs, his family and mine,
their fixed improbable faces.

                                        Eventually,
we find the general store, the left-turn fork,
the hidden waterfall still
battering the rocks,
and the ease of recognition makes me old.
Standing close enough to feel the spray,
looking up at the falls, its powerful
inexhaustible rush of water,
I think that art has ruined my life,
fraught as it is with what's exceptional.

But that's not true; at the start, at nineteen,
I wanted it all,
every exhilaration, every grief—

acquisitive was what he said.
How could I have hurt him?
Such a new candle, just lit, burning, burning.

Memorial Day

In field guides they are always in repose:
tiny female, olive-gray, so like the local birds;
the male, shiny black with tailstripes, wingbars,
"shoulder coloration" such a vivid orange
I might have recognized him in the elm.
But this close—for days, midday, over and over
they sprang from the nearest branch of the shrub,
slinging themselves at the glass, then hovering there
with so much apparent purpose my son said,
Why don't you open the window and let them in?

For a moment, it was the voice of clearest reason.
And it must have been the same for the early fishermen
on the Klamath River, after
the terrible dark winters of retribution,
seeing the water clot with fish and fish twist
willingly into their nets, who thought the salmon
had been sent to feed them and their families—
hadn't they prayed steadily, and weren't the fish
laboring upstream?
                                        Likewise, my father's cousin,
deep in the mud and confusion of the war,
heard a woman's voice, distinct
as a mouthharp, his dead wife's voice,
urging him out of the foxhole, out of the path
of the sudden German shell that killed the others.
And now, two rare impatient birds flying at me, erect,
sun-struck, treading the air, their mouths propped
open as if to speak, as if they were not birds
but messengers—
                                    but I am overrun with signs and omens:
the pair death has taken
swim up like motes in my eye, I find them

everywhere I look, I put them there; it is a blindness.
American redstart warblers. If they have meaning, perhaps
they represent the living, not the dead;
and I am meant to understand
death is locked behind the glass
that teases with our own reflections
until the implicating sun moves to the southwest
and the window once again holds only shadow.

It's been a week since their last visitation.
At the window, the smudge of purple,
those small rich berries the buds made,
has opened into the blossoms'
distinguishing pastel, a thicket of lilac.
From time to time I catch among the usual calls
a sequence of notes—not a warble at all but abrupt
chips of sound—to match the guide's
approximating graph, which records,
though it cannot translate, what they say.

The Wish

My daughter comes to me
with her sorrow. She is
not yet ten, not yet
insistent for her father.
As if waiting out a sentence,
she sits at the round table,
her long black shawl of hair
framing high cheekbones.
She thinks she is ugly,
thinks she has no friends.

How can I comfort, what should I
try to tell this radiant
coincidence of genes?
That children can be beasts
to one another? That envy
eats us from the inside?
"All great beauties
doubted their beauty," I tell her.
But why should she believe me:
I am her mother, and asked
repeatedly for beauty,
meaning happiness.

Bright Leaf

Like words put to a song, the bunched tobacco leaves
are strung along a stick, the women
standing in the August heat for hours—since first light—
under the pitched tin roof, barefoot, and at their feet
the babies, bare-assed, dirty, eating dirt.
The older children hand the leaves from the slide,
three leaves at a time, stalks upright, three handers
for each stringer, and three more heaped canvas slides
waiting in what little shade there is: it's ten o'clock,
almost dinnertime. They pull the pails of cold lunch
and Mason jars of tea out of the spring
when they see the farmer coming from the field, their men
stripped to the waist, polished by sweat and tired as mules.
By afternoon, the loose cotton dresses, even
the headrags are dark with sweat.
Still their fingers never miss a stitch,
though they're paid not by the stick but by the day,
and the talk—unbroken news of cousins and acquaintances—
unwinding with the ball of twine, a frayed snuff-twig
bouncing on one lip, the string paying out
through their calluses, the piles of wide green leaves
diminishing, until the men appear with the last slide
and clamber up the rafters of the barn
to line the loaded sticks along the tiers. It's Friday:

the farmer pays with a wad of ones and fives,
having turned the mule out to its feed and water,
hung up the stiffened traces and the bit. He checks
again the other barns, already fired, crude ovens
of log and mud where the crop is cured;
in that hot dry acrid air, spreads a yellowing leaf
across his palm, rolls an edge in his fingers,
gauging by its texture and its smell
how high to drive the fire.

His crew is quiet in the pickup truck—did you think
they were singing? They are much too tired to even speak,
can barely lick salt from the back of a hand, brush at flies,
hush a baby with a sugartit. And the man
who owns this land is also tired.
Everyday this week he's meant to bring home pears
from the old tree by the barn, but now he sees
the fruit has fallen, sees the yellow jackets feeding there.
He lights a Lucky, frames a joke for his wife—he'll say
their banker raised a piss-poor field this year.
And she will lean against the doorjamb
while he talks, while he scrubs his hands at the tin basin
with a split lemon and a pumice stone, rubs them raw
trying to cut the gummy resin, that stubborn
black stain within the green.

The Fence

Think of it as a target's outer edge—
the bands of lawn, gravel, lawn,
the red brick bull's-eye of the house.
Dead center was the kitchen, whose windows opened
a view of the yard, the trees and bushes
newly planted, each in its small depression,
and the more ambitious birds—
cardinal, blue jay, mockingbird—
tagging the older trees beside the fence.
Along one flank of the yard, that meant mimosa,
a pink canopy, silk blossoms shaped
like downy parasols; and it was here
she taught herself to move beyond the branches
onto the edge, inching down the planks
around the house. When she fell
she fell inward, away from the field.
But once in the air and moving forward,
she was neither in the yard nor in the field,
balanced over hay and broom,
the dried plates of dung and piles
still liquid, green as infection, the hidden
nests of snakes or rabbits, and the obvious cows,
wearing their stockings of offal, lurching and switching.
How easily the world was once divided. In the field
the doves cried in their private tunnels of grass,
and beyond, her father's pasture gave way
to woods and creek, the high trestle,
someone else's woods and creek. She knew
who was supposed to be the sun, who the moon,
who the pebble under the skirt of the moon.
By summer's end, doubling her own height
she'd traced the whole decorative length of wood
around the house to the corner by the road
where fence was used to keep things in, not out.

And that is how I see her even now
not yet straining against a tether but held erect
by the gravitational pull from either side—
face forward, arms extended, headed for the far post
where wood turned into wire.

Equinox

The garden slackens under frost,
and the trees, scored by the season's extravagant
orange and red, begin discarding
what they will not need.
How many more signals do we want?
Brown, gray, the brown skittery refuse in the field
is what the natural world is moving toward.
In the middle distance,
the children run to the creek,
run to the dwarf-apple and across
the clipped green grass to where their father
is stacking wood, all of them wearing primary blue.
This yard is what we salvage from the scrub
that overtakes the orchard and the pasture.
Perennial. The earth mocks us,
and in the blue heavens,
nothing visible
but her pale oblivious twin.

Landscape, Dense with Trees

When you move away, you see how much depends
on the pace of the days—how much
depended on the haze we waded through
each summer, visible heat, wavy and discursive
as the lazy track of the snake in the dusty road;
and on the habit in town of porches thatched in vines,
and in the country long dense promenades, the way
we sacrificed the yards to shade.
It was partly the heat that made my father
plant so many trees—two maples marking the site
for the house, two elms on either side when it was done;
mimosa by the fence, and as it failed, fast-growing chestnuts,
loblolly pines; and dogwood, redbud, ornamental crab.
On the farm, everything else he grew
something could eat, but this
would be a permanent mark of his industry,
a glade established in the open field. Or so it seemed.
Looking back at the empty house from across the hill,
I see how well the house is camouflaged, see how
that porous fence of saplings, their later
scrim of foliage, thickened around it,
and still he chinked and mortared, planting more.
Last summer, although he'd lost all tolerance for heat,
he backed the truck in at the family grave
and stood in the truckbed all afternoon, pruning
the landmark oak, repairing recent damage by a wind;
then he came home and hung a swing
in one of the horse-chestnuts for my visit.
The heat was a hand at his throat,
a fist to his weak heart. But it made a triumph
of the cooler air inside, in the bedroom,
in the maple bedstead where he slept,
in the brick house nearly swamped by leaves.

The Lotus Flowers

The surface of the pond was mostly green—
bright green algae reaching out from the banks,
then the mass of waterlilies, their broad round leaves
rim to rim, each white flower spreading
from the center of a green saucer.
We teased and argued, choosing the largest,
the sweetest bloom, but when the rowboat
lumbered through and rearranged them,
we found the plants were anchored, the separate
muscular stems descending in the dense water—
only the most determined put her hand
into that frog-slimed pond
to wrestle with a flower. Back and forth
we pumped across the water, in twos and threes,
full of brave adventure. On the marshy shore,
the others hollered for their turns,
or at the hem of where we pitched the tents
gathered firewood—

this was wilderness,
although the pond was less than half an acre
and we could still see the grand magnolias
in the village cemetary, their waxy
white conical blossoms gleaming in the foliage.
A dozen girls, the oldest only twelve, two sisters
with their long braids, my shy neighbor,
someone squealing without interruption:
all we didn't know about the world buoyed us,
as the frightful water sustained and moved the flowers
tethered at a depth we couldn't see.

In the late afternoon, before they'd folded
into candles on the dark water,
I went to fill the bucket at the spring.

Deep in the pines, exposed tree roots
formed a natural arch, a cave of black loam.
I raked off the skin of leaves and needles,
leaving a pool so clear and shallow
I could count the pebbles
on the studded floor. The sudden cold
splashing up from the bucket to my hands
made me want to plunge my hand in—
and I held it under, feeling the shock that wakes
and deadens, watching first my fingers,
then the ledge beyond me,
the snake submerged and motionless,
the head propped on its coils the way a girl
crosses her arms before her on the sill
and rests her chin there.
                                        Lugging the bucket
back to the noisy clearing, I found nothing changed,
the boat still rocked across the pond,
the fire straggled and cracked as we fed it
branches and debris into the night,
leaning back on our pallets—
spokes in a wheel—learning the names of the many
constellations, learning how each fixed
cluster took its name:
not from the strongest light, but from the pattern
made by stars of lesser magnitude,
so like the smaller stars we rowed among.

May

Raccoons on the porch, the deer
leaving stenciled hearts
in the soft ground beneath the apple tree—
yesterday Will announced
"a wild and beautiful goose" up the brook.
I thought it must have been a duck
but today, looking out the back window
toward the stream, I see
what I take to be a pile of trash
until it moves—
                                        there is a goose,
preening its long neck, its orange lips
grazing among the cress and mown grass,
though for minutes at a time it doesn't move.

In the painting that our yard would be,
the blunt white goose pulls the eye
from the white circle of the blossoming tree—
it lights the tree,
as if its smaller swatch of white
conjured brilliance out of the shadowed grass.

One by one I call the others;
we stand together, watching, in a hush.
And so it is
when the dog drags home the plush
hindquarter of a deer; or when
a single beaver sits beside the barn,
holding up his paws like a friendly dog.

Dancing with Poets

"The accident" is what he calls the time
he threw himself from a window four floors up,
breaking his back and both ankles, so that walking
became the direst labor for this man
who takes my hand, invites me to the empty strip of floor
that fronts the instruments, a length of polished wood
the shape of a grave. *Unsuited for this world—*
his body bears the marks of it, his hand
is tense with effort and with shame, and I shy away
from any audience, but I love to dance, and soon
we find a way to move, drifting apart as each
effects a different ripple across the floor,
a plaid and a stripe to match the solid navy of the band.
And suddenly the band is getting better, so pleased
to have this pair of dancers, since we make evident
the music in the noise—and the dull pulse
leaps with unexpected riffs and turns, we can hear
how good the keyboard really is, the bright cresting
of another major key as others join us: a strict
block of a man, a formidable cliff of mind, dancing
as if melted, as if unhinged; his partner a gift of brave
elegance to those who watch her dance; and at her elbow,
Berryman back from the bridge, and Frost, relieved
of grievances, Dickinson waltzing there with lavish Keats,
who coughs into a borrowed handkerchief—all the poets of exile
and despair, unfit for this life, all those who cannot speak
but only sing, all those who cannot walk
who strut and spin until the waiting citizens at the bar,
aloof, judgmental, begin to sway or drum their straws
or hum, leave their seats to crowd the narrow floor

and now we are one body, sweating and foolish,
one body with its clear pathetic grace, not
lifted out of grief but dancing it, transforming
for one night this local bar, before we're turned back out
to our separate selves, to the dangerous streets and houses,
to the overwhelming drone of the living world.

THE AUTHOR

ELLEN BRYANT VOIGT grew up in Virginia, graduated from Converse College, and received an M.F.A. from the University of Iowa. The author of two previous collections of poems, *Claiming Kin* (1976) and *The Forces of Plenty* (1983), she has received grants from the National Endowment for the Arts and the Guggenheim Foundation. A former faculty member at Goddard College and M.I.T., she currently teaches in the Warren Wilson College low-residency M.F.A. Program for Writers. She lives in Cabot, Vermont, with her husband and two children.